Ants

by Nancy Tyler
illustrated by Steve Henry

Core Decodable 10

McGraw Hill Education

Bothell, WA • Chicago, IL • Columbus, OH • New York, NY

MHEonline.com

Send all inquiries to:
McGraw-Hill Education
8787 Orion Place
Columbus, OH 43240

ISBN: 978-0-02-145716-8
MHID: 0-02-145716-6

Printed in the United States of America.

7 8 9 LCR 25 24 23

Nat and Nan sat.

Nat and Nan stand.

Nat and Nan stand and stand.

Ants see Nat and Nan.

Nat and Nan sat.

Nan and Nat see ants!